D1575487

For:

_____

You've been
a blessing to me!

From:

_____

Teachers Are a Gift from God
Copyright 2001 by Zondervan
ISBN 0-310-80252-0

Requests for information should be addressed to:
Inspirio, the gift group of Zondervan
Grand Rapids, Michigan 49530
http://www.inspiriogifts.com

Project Manager: Molly Detweiler
Compiler: Pat Matuszak
Design: Kimberly Visser

Printed in China
03 04 05 /HK / 4 3 2

Teachers are a Gift from God

inspirio™

Teaching takes time &

   energy, paying

   attention to all the

Children,

helping them,

   encouraging them,

reaching out to the quiet one, &

   Sometimes simply being there.

*W*herever they go, teachers always hear a little voice in their minds wondering, How can I use that in my class? They go to conferences looking for ideas and inspiration from other teachers. They watch television and movies and make little notes about ideas they see. One day Angela, a teacher friend of mine, and I were shopping at a garden center and she enlisted me, and two sales ladies, to try to catch a small lizard that was hiding in some plants. She wanted to take it back to school and surprise her fourth graders on Monday. (I drew the line at trapping it in my new purse.)

PAT MATUSZAK

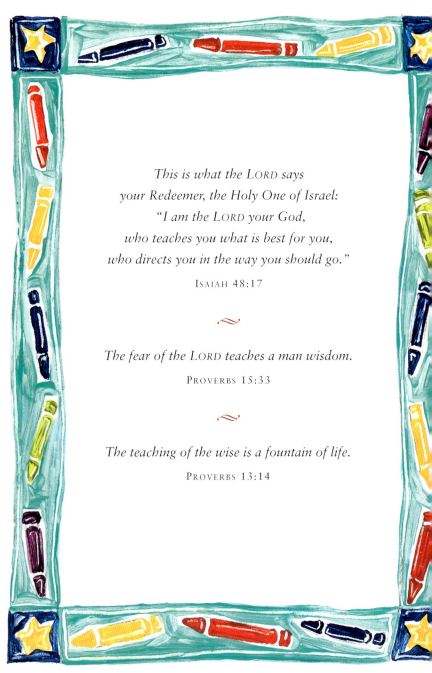

*This is what the L*ORD *says*
your Redeemer, the Holy One of Israel:
*"I am the L*ORD *your God,*
who teaches you what is best for you,
who directs you in the way you should go."

ISAIAH 48:17

*The fear of the L*ORD *teaches a man wisdom.*

PROVERBS 15:33

The teaching of the wise is a fountain of life.

PROVERBS 13:14

*I*n the ranks of music history, my seventh-grade music instructor will probably occupy the halls of obscurity, but in my memory he shines.

Mr. Strang wasn't a virtuoso clarinetist and I don't believe he even played the saxophone, the instrument I studied under him. He was a master, however, at the art of encouragement. I can still hear his voice after just about any of those long-ago, fumbling first lessons: *Bob, great job. As always, it's been a pleasure.*

He really meant it. Amazing! You can pay for instruction. What you can't purchase is inspiration, and that is what my first music instructor gave me. He lit in me a spark that never went out, a love for music that's remained strong through the years. The first thing I learned from Richard Strang was the fingering for the note D. But his greatest, most enduring lesson has been the power of encouraging words to ignite vision and possibility, the best and the highest, within another person. Thank you, Mr. Strang!

BOB HARTIG

As a baby, I had lost several fingers on my right hand through a severe car accident. The deformity never bothered me—and certainly never stopped me from getting my hands into everything—until I attended school. School kids taught me quickly the value of slipping my hand behind my back, keeping it in my pocket whenever possible, and stretching my sleeves so my hand could wriggle into a hiding place while still holding a book. I didn't care about not having fingers—I could still play the piano and ride my bike—but I did care about looking different.

One day, in grade three, my teacher came to my desk and whispered that the principal would like to see me in his office before I went out for recess that day. Now, I was scared of my principal. I sat in my desk seat staring at the clock, feeling suddenly very hot.

When recess came, I faced the inevitable. I said goodbye to my best friend, who promised to pray for me. I knocked on the door, expecting to see Mr. Kloster's stern eyes on the other side of the glass, staring into me.

Strangely, Mr. Kloster smiled and beckoned me in.

"Have a seat, Heather. I'm so glad you could come." I didn't reciprocate the feeling; instead, I looked at the floor.

"Heather, I know you've been attending this school for the last three years, but I hadn't noticed a certain something special about you until last week. And when I did, I realized that we have something in common."

I looked up at him and he held up a deformed hand. My eyes must have gone buggy because Mr. Kloster laughed. "You didn't notice it about me either, then, eh? I guess we're even." He had a nice laugh.

After that we told each other our stories, sharing some of the frustrations of our handicap. I soon forgot all about my best friend and stayed with Mr. Kloster the entire recess. It was the bell that called our conversation to a close. As I was about to leave, Mr. Kloster said, "You're a beautiful young girl, Heather. I'm glad we have something in common."

I smiled and was glad too.

HEATHER GEMMEN

9

I took our fourth- and fifth-graders to the symphony today. It tickled me to look over and see two fourth grade boys with a copy of the instrument family color sheets that we completed in music class. They were diligently searching the orchestra for each instrument listed or illustrated on their page. It was very impressive that it was important enough to the boys to bring the sheets with them.

CHLOE, A FOURTH GRADE MUSIC TEACHER

Train a child in the way
he should go, and when he is old
he will not turn from it.

PROVERBS 22:6

Come, my children, listen to me;
I will teach you
the fear of the LORD.

PSALM 34:11

The wise in heart are called discerning,
and pleasant words promote instruction.

PROVERBS 16:21

One of the things that I have learned after being a home school mom for many years is that learning is not confined to the textbook. Some of our best "teachable moments" have occurred when doing an ordinary task which suddenly presents an incredible opportunity for an object lesson.

One such opportunity presented itself when my five-year-old daughter and I were outside doing some yard work. While I was pulling weeds, my daughter was busy filling a bucket with water, using the hose. After the bucket was full, she would dump it out in the driveway and start over.

After watching her do this three or four times, I decided that it was time for a lesson in ecology and stewardship of the earth's resources. I proceeded to explain to her that dumping the water in the driveway was wasting it, and that if she wanted to have fun filling the bucket, she should use the water by dumping it in the garden or the flowerbed. She understood, and so ended the lesson—so I thought. That night as I was tucking her into bed she said, "Mom, if God doesn't use me before I die, will I be wasted?" Stunned by such a deep thought for such a little girl, I was momentarily without a response.

"Where did you hear that?" was all I could muster. "I just thought of it. You know how if you dump a bucket of water out without using it it's wasted?" she asked.

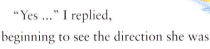

"Yes ..." I replied, beginning to see the direction she was coming from.

"Well, it's the same with people, you know? God made us, and someday we're going to die. And if God doesn't use me before I die will I be wasted?"

We went on to have the most precious talk about God's plan for her life, and how I was sure that God would use her! He already had! I was awestruck at how God had taken a simple lesson and turned it into a deep spiritual truth in a little girl's heart. We never know how God will use what we teach, and from that moment on I had a much deeper respect for the awesome privilege and responsibility that I held as the teacher of children.

LORI

13

Some Letters from Kids:

Mr. Rozek:

Thank you for being a great teacher. You were very patient with me and I appreciate that. Thanks for everything.

FROM CHRISTINA

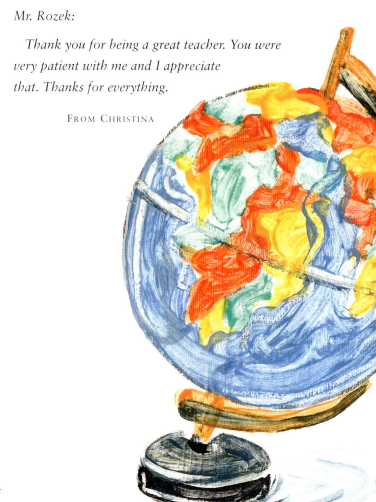

Before I met Mr. Rozek I had a real tough time with teachers. I was always scared of them. But when I was a freshman and I had Mr. Rozek he changed everything for me. He made the class fun and interactive. He gave and we gave. He was personable. He made me glad to go to school! Before, I thought I was dumb. But Mr. Rozek made work fun! Believe it or not he made me love Shakespeare!

From Mr. Rozek I learned that teachers are people (so naturally I lost my fear). I also learned that I am not dumb.

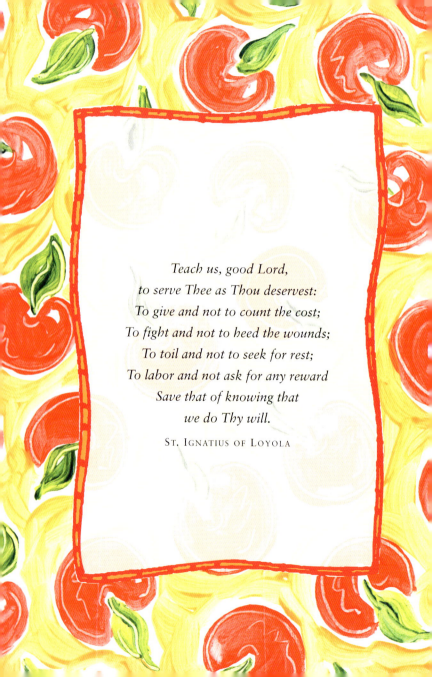

Teach us, good Lord,
to serve Thee as Thou deservest:
To give and not to count the cost;
To fight and not to heed the wounds;
To toil and not to seek for rest;
To labor and not ask for any reward
Save that of knowing that
we do Thy will.

ST. IGNATIUS OF LOYOLA

One of the best examples of patient encouragement I ever witnessed was that of sixth-grade band director Jim Mollema. One day during the first weeks of school, I was passing the band room on the way to my classroom when I heard a screeching noise that sounded as if it could only have been made by the simultaneous violent deaths of dozens of unfortunate cats. Then the screeching stopped just as I passed the door.

Peeking in unobserved, I saw Jim standing at the director's podium with his baton lightly poised as he addressed a class of about fifty sixth-graders, proudly holding various band instruments in their laps.

"That was very nice," he said in his gentle, calm voice with genuine enthusiasm. One would have thought the aural assault the students had just produced was the sound he had been waiting to hear all his life. "Now let's go back to the top and try that again, shall we?" he smiled.

This man gained my undying respect as he repeated the same loving exercise every day for the whole year.

PAT MATUSZAK

One of the funniest moments that happened to me as an elementary teacher was when I ran into several third-grade students at the local grocery store. They looked at me with disbelief for a moment; then one of them finally exclaimed, "Mrs. Matuszak! You buy groceries!" I guess they had never thought of a teacher having a life outside of the classroom.

PAT MATUSZAK

A builder built a temple
        He wrought with care and skill.
Pillars and joints and arches
        Were fashioned to meet his will;
And men said when they saw its beauty:
        "It shall never know decay.
Great is thy skill, O builder,
        Thy fame shall endure for thee."
A teacher built a temple;
        She wrought with skill and care,
Forming each pillar with patience,
        Laying each stone with prayer.
None saw the unceasing effort;
        None knew of the marvelous plan;
For the temple the teacher built
        Was unseen by the eyes of man.
Gone is the builder's temple;
        Crumbled into the dust,
Pillar and joint and arches
        Food for consuming rust;
But the temple the teacher built
        Shall endure while the ages roll;
For that beautiful, unseen temple
        Was a child's immortal soul.

AUTHOR UNKNOWN

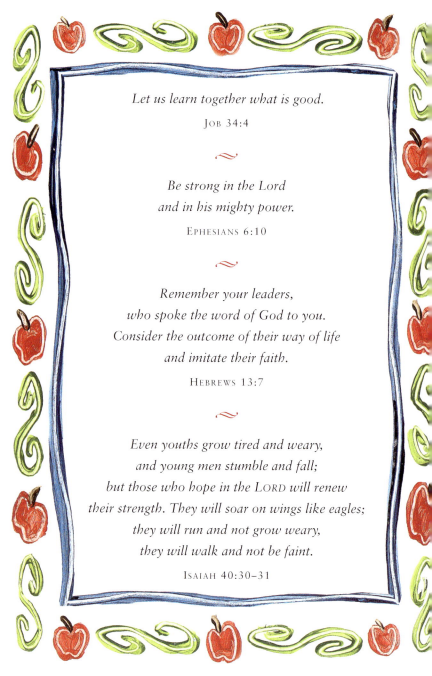

Let us learn together what is good.

JOB 34:4

*Be strong in the Lord
and in his mighty power.*

EPHESIANS 6:10

*Remember your leaders,
who spoke the word of God to you.
Consider the outcome of their way of life
and imitate their faith.*

HEBREWS 13:7

*Even youths grow tired and weary,
and young men stumble and fall;
but those who hope in the LORD will renew
their strength. They will soar on wings like eagles;
they will run and not grow weary,
they will walk and not be faint.*

ISAIAH 40:30–31

$\mathcal{M}$ ost teachers looking back will say they had a horrible first year! But they also will advise that teaching gets easier as each year passes and that they learn at least as much from the experiences as do their students. They are befriended by teaching mentors and learn to ask many and frequent questions everywhere and of everyone. They quit trying to be perfect when they realize that students will learn as much from mistakes as from letter-perfect, planned lessons.

ANN

At the end of what had probably been one of the worst mornings of a truly discouraging week in the classroom, I dragged into the teachers' lounge to collapse for my lunch break. I didn't have much hope that even the high-test, teacher-strength coffee from the giant lounge percolator would be able to energize me to return to my classroom when the bell rang. When I reached the coffee counter, I found a surprise that just made my day, and I went back to my room with new hope. There was a red wicker basket full of cookies and apples. A flowered note card attached to the handle read: "Dear Teachers: We are praying for you today! God bless you, Moms in Touch."

PAT MATUSZAK

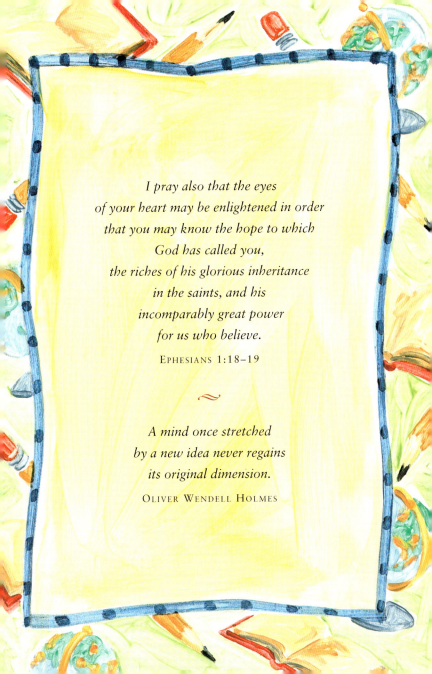

I pray also that the eyes
of your heart may be enlightened in order
that you may know the hope to which
God has called you,
the riches of his glorious inheritance
in the saints, and his
incomparably great power
for us who believe.

EPHESIANS 1:18–19

A mind once stretched
by a new idea never regains
its original dimension.

OLIVER WENDELL HOLMES

*D*evelop a sixth sense about your students. Learn to tell when they are having a bad day, and give them the space they need to cope with it. One piece of advice an assistant principal gave me my first day on the job was, "It is easier to lighten up than to tighten up." So far that has proven true for me. Each class knows on day one what I will tolerate, and everyone gets along a whole lot better because of it. Kids hate surprises.

Mrs. B

Advice to new teachers:
Don't smile for the first six weeks.

Old teacher saying

Teach me, my God and King,
In all things thee to see;
Teach me to be in every-
thing;
All thou wouldst have
me be.

In all I think or say,
Lord,
May I not offend.
In all I do, be thou the
way;
In all be thou the end.

Each task I undertake,
Though weak and mean to me,
If undertaken for thy sake;
Draws strength and worth from thee.

Teach me, then, Lord, to bring,
To all that I may be,
To all I do, my God and King,
A consciousness of thee.

Change starts with one person. Any candle we light does make the darkness a little less. Here's to lighting those candles!

I have never given up on people in all of these years. I once learned that I should look for the good in all people. I try to do that. That keeps me optimistic because I usually am able to find at least a shred of goodness in the people I meet!

I only wish that I could eliminate prejudice. I wish people would realize they are more alike than they are different. Bottom line—we are all in this thing called life together; we should work together to make it the best we can and perhaps to leave it in a little better shape than it was.

Here's to remaining positive and to making a difference!

I am a veteran teacher (thirty-two years), and if I can be of any help, I will do what I can! Opening the doors for students is so important!

As for discipline, everyone has his or her own style, but I can tell you what has worked for me, and I have very few discipline problems. I basically treat students the way I would want to be treated. I treat them with respect, and they give it back to me. I am very open with them, too. I tell them that I care about them, and because I care, I work hard to make sure they have skills; however, I also tell them that it is their decision whether or not they are going to be successful. It has worked for me. I guess the big thing is establishing a rapport with your students. They need to know that you are human, too!

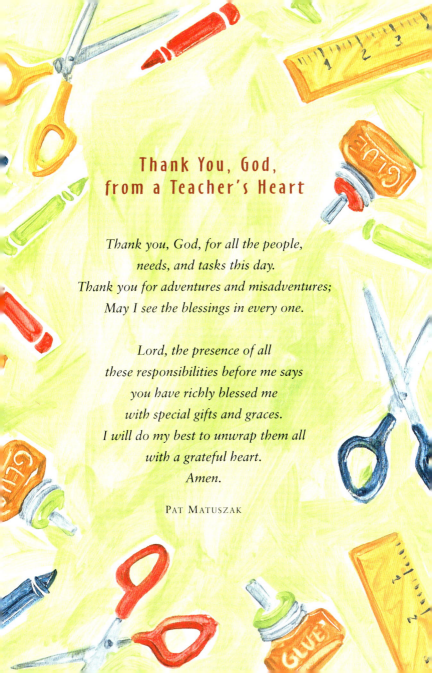

Thank You, God, from a Teacher's Heart

Thank you, God, for all the people,
needs, and tasks this day.
Thank you for adventures and misadventures;
May I see the blessings in every one.

Lord, the presence of all
these responsibilities before me says
you have richly blessed me
with special gifts and graces.
I will do my best to unwrap them all
with a grateful heart.
Amen.

PAT MATUSZAK

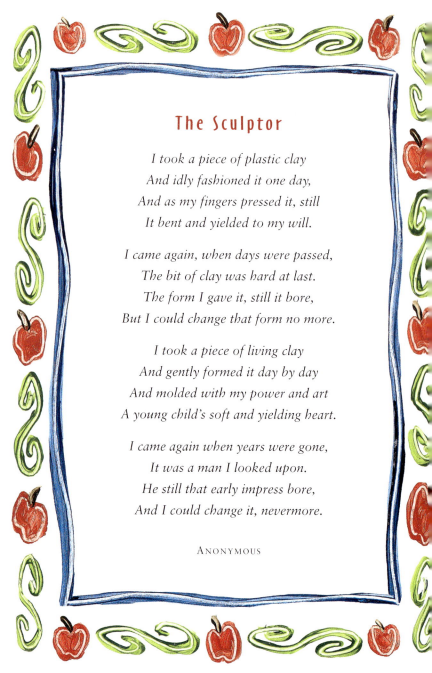

The Sculptor

I took a piece of plastic clay
And idly fashioned it one day,
And as my fingers pressed it, still
It bent and yielded to my will.

I came again, when days were passed,
The bit of clay was hard at last.
The form I gave it, still it bore,
But I could change that form no more.

I took a piece of living clay
And gently formed it day by day
And molded with my power and art
A young child's soft and yielding heart.

I came again when years were gone,
It was a man I looked upon.
He still that early impress bore,
And I could change it, nevermore.

ANONYMOUS

A teacher effects eternity;
he can never tell where his influence stops.

HENRY B. ADAMS

～

He who opens a school door, closes a prison.

VICTOR HUGO

～

If you can read this, thank a teacher.

BUMPER STICKER

～

Education is not the filling of a pail,
but the lighting of a fire.

WILLIAM BUTLER YEATS

Who is wise and understanding among
you? Let him show it by his good life,
by deeds done in the humility
that comes from wisdom.

JAMES 3:13

~

A wise man's heart guides his mouth,
and his lips promote instruction.

PROVERBS 16:23

~

Apply your heart to instruction
and your ears to words of knowledge.

PROVERBS 23:12

Be kind and compassionate to one another,
forgiving each other, just as in Christ God forgave you.

EPHESIANS 4:32

Do to others as you would have them do to you.

LUKE 6:31

"Fix these words of mine in your hearts and minds,"
says the LORD, *"tie them as symbols on your hands*
and bind them on your foreheads.
Teach them to your children, talking about them
when you sit at home and when you walk along the road,
when you lie down and when you get up."

DEUTERONOMY 11:18–19

We proclaim Christ,
admonishing and teaching everyone
with all wisdom, so that
we may present everyone perfect in Christ.

COLOSSIANS 1:28

~

It was God who gave some to be apostles,
some to be prophets, some to be evangelists,
and some to be pastors and teachers,
to prepare God's people for works of service,
so that the body of Christ may be built up
until we all reach unity in the faith
and in the knowledge of the Son of God
and become mature, attaining to
the whole measure of the fullness of Christ.

EPHESIANS 4:11–13

The great Master said, "I see
No best in kind, but in degree;
I gave various gifts to each,
To charm, to strengthen, and to teach."

HENRY WADSWORTH LONGFELLOW

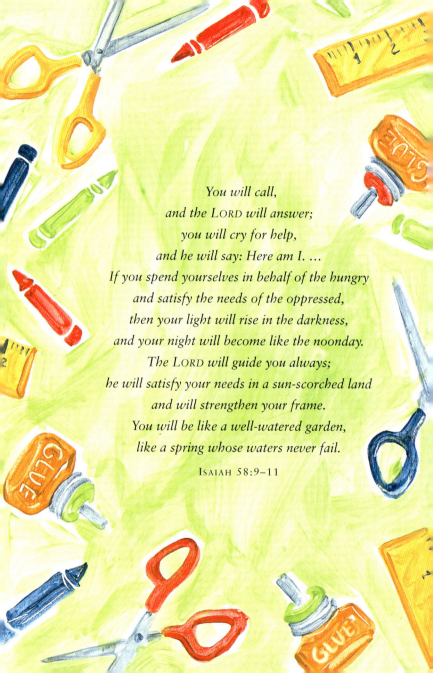

You will call,
and the LORD will answer;
you will cry for help,
and he will say: Here am I. …
If you spend yourselves in behalf of the hungry
and satisfy the needs of the oppressed,
then your light will rise in the darkness,
and your night will become like the noonday.
The LORD will guide you always;
he will satisfy your needs in a sun-scorched land
and will strengthen your frame.
You will be like a well-watered garden,
like a spring whose waters never fail.

ISAIAH 58:9–11

Know that
the LORD is God.
It is he who made us, and we are his;
we are his people, the sheep of his pasture.
Enter his gates with thanksgiving
and his courts with praise;
give thanks to him and praise his name.
For the LORD is good
and his love endures forever;
his faithfulness continues
through all generations.

PSALM 100:3–5

The most important element for teachers is that you like children—because kids know when they are liked, and they know when they are not. The eyes of children see beyond masks and professional manners—they see the real you. Love your work. Cherish your sense of humor and enjoy the little ones entrusted to your care.

Mrs. G

O LORD, you have searched me
and you know me.
You know when I sit and when I rise;
you perceive my thoughts from afar.

PSALM 139:1–2

Let me understand
the teaching of your precepts;
then I will meditate
on your wonders, O LORD.

PSALM 119:27

The discerning heart seeks knowledge.

PROVERBS 15:14

The true teacher defends his pupils
against his own personal influence.
He inspires self-trust.
He guides their eyes from himself
to the spirit that quickens him.

AMOS BRONSON ALCOTT

Delightful task! to rear the tender thought,
To teach the young idea how to shoot.

JAMES THOMSON

No matter what rosy picture the movies or books portray about teaching, we cannot reach every student. We may only see the results of our work years later, rather than before a semester ends. Once in a while a student realizes the help he or she was given in the classroom and calls or comes back to visit—those are the golden moments. But often the teacher never hears a thank you. We just have to have faith that the fledglings we fed, then pushed from the nest have gone on to safe havens with the skills we taught.

TOM

The teacher I'll always remember was my senior high English teacher, Helen Fitting. She just loved reading and words. When she would read us a new selection, the expression on her face was as though she were tasting double-chocolate cheesecake! Then she'd just smile and look around the room for a few seconds and see if anyone else caught the experience. We very often did and developed a "taste" for literature. She taught us to love words.

PAT MATUSZAK

*A teacher who can arouse
a feeling for one single good action,
for one single good poem,
accomplishes more than he who fills our memory
with rows on rows of natural objects,
classified with name and form.*

JOHANN WOLFGANG VON GOETHE

*Instruct a wise man
and he will be wiser still;
teach a righteous man
and he will add to his learning.*

PROVERBS 9:9

No one has yet realized
the wealth of sympathy, the kindness
and generosity, hidden in the soul of a child.
The effort of every true education should be
to unlock that treasure.

EMMA GOLDMAN

⌒

Jesus said,
"Whoever humbles himself like this child
is the greatest in the kingdom of heaven.
And whoever welcomes
a little child like this in my name
welcomes me."

MATTHEW 18:4–5

Some excerpts from a paper written by a little girl about her teacher:

Mr. Alexander was my fifth-grade teacher. He was really nice. Mr. Alexander was tall, really smart, funny and nice.

His favorite subject was writing or language arts. He taught us how to use a writing pyramid. How to write detailed sentences.

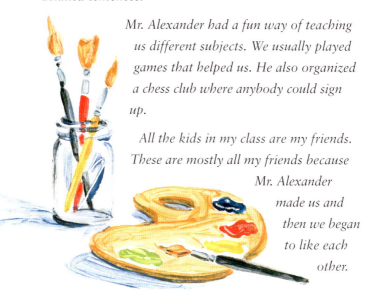

Mr. Alexander had a fun way of teaching us different subjects. We usually played games that helped us. He also organized a chess club where anybody could sign up.

All the kids in my class are my friends. These are mostly all my friends because Mr. Alexander made us and then we began to like each other.

In everything set them an example
by doing what is good.
In your teaching show integrity,
seriousness and soundness of speech.

TITUS 2:7–8

Jesus said, "Knock and the door
will be opened to you.
For everyone who asks receives;
he who seeks finds; and to him who knocks,
the door will be opened."

MATTHEW 7:7–8

"I guide you in the way of wisdom
and lead you along straight paths,"
says the LORD.

PROVERBS 4:11

Wisdom is sweet to your soul;
if you find it, there is a future hope for you.

PROVERBS 24:14

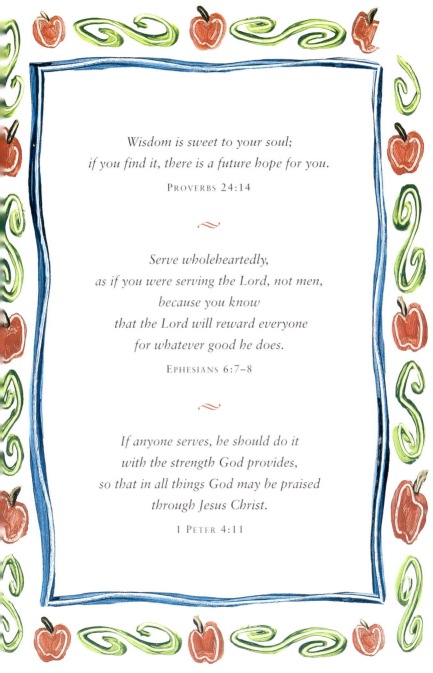

Serve wholeheartedly,
as if you were serving the Lord, not men,
because you know
that the Lord will reward everyone
for whatever good he does.

EPHESIANS 6:7–8

If anyone serves, he should do it
with the strength God provides,
so that in all things God may be praised
through Jesus Christ.

1 PETER 4:11

The very spring and root of honesty and virtue lie in a good education.

Does the place you're called to labor
Seem too small and little known?
It is great if God is in it,
And He'll not forget His own.

Little is much when God is in it!
Labor not for wealth or fame.
There's a crown—and you can win it,
If you go in Jesus' Name.

KITTIE L. SUFFIELD

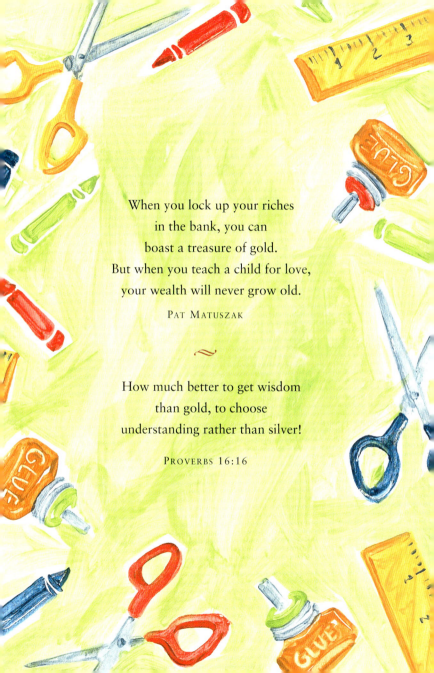

When you lock up your riches
in the bank, you can
boast a treasure of gold.
But when you teach a child for love,
your wealth will never grow old.

Pat Matuszak

~

How much better to get wisdom
than gold, to choose
understanding rather than silver!

Proverbs 16:16

SOURCES

Thank you to friends and colleagues who contributed stories to this collection.

Matuszak, Pat. *Teacher Stories*.

At Inspirio we love to hear from you—your stories, your feedback,
and your product ideas.
Please send your comments to us
by way of e-mail at
icares@zondervan.com
or to the address below:

inspirio

Attn: Inspirio Cares
5300 Patterson Avenue SE
Grand Rapids, MI 49530

If you would like further information
about Inspirio and the products we
create please visit us at:
www.inspiriogifts.com

Thank you and God Bless!